dillieroad.com

She Sings Only When I'm Naked

by
Christopher Garrett

♪

a mélange of
translucent moments
in poetry and prose

All poems and prose in this book are the sole work of the author. No AI was used in the creation of any of these writings. Of note: the use of em dashes is the author's stylistic choice to promote clarity and emphasis. He refuses to let the abuse proliferated by AI algorithms dictate his preferences for punctuation.

The author's desire is that the reader will experience the poems and prose in this book on a personal level. He seeks to respect all people, and this includes being aware of how pronouns in his writings may affect a reader's personalization of the message. When possible, he uses inclusive pronouns. However, there are some poems in which message and flow would be compromised by avoidance of specific pronouns. In such instances, he asks the reader to simply replace in their mind the written pronoun with the pronoun of their choice.

She Sings Only When I'm Naked

Copyright ©2025 by Christopher Garrett

All rights reserved. This book or any portion thereof may not be reproduced or used in any manner whatsoever without the express written permission of the publisher, except for the use of brief quotations in a book review.

NO AI TRAINING: Without in any way limiting the author's and Dillie Road Books' exclusive rights under copyright, any use of this publication to "train" generative artificial intelligence (AI) technologies to generate text is expressly prohibited. The author reserves all rights to license any and all uses of this work for generative AI training and development of machine learning language models.

ISBN: 978-1-7379040-3-8

First published in the United States by Dillie Road Books

www.dillieroad.com

www.christophergarrett.co

Prologue

In my 45-year quest to pluck each day (the more literal translation of *carpe diem* better represents my attempts), she has never feigned the courtesy of a knock. She flings the door wide open, entering without invocation, and there I stand in all my exposed glory—a euphemism if ever there was.

She always mandates that I remain utterly uncovered, no matter if I am bleeding or blubbering or belittling or boasting. And I wait—unprotected, bare—knowing she will thrust into my soul that ubiquitous blade which serves as sword and scalpel: the conjugal union of words. Unions concocting potions, narcotics, tonics, and antidotes. Words without promise to euthanize, heal, or resuscitate—only to pierce the soul and discover whether life remains.

I possess ample delusion and defiance and desperation (yes, I'm a slave to alliteration) to have put pen to paper, persisting many of our moments. Herein are the ensuing poems and prose—the relics of our encounters. I'm quite confident she cares not that I'm revealing them to you as she has nothing to hide and no need for the delusion of decorum.

The pages will not provide a gentle journey, but they will afford a meaningful voyage. I have comingled these relics with but tepid efforts at courteous continuity. Only a charlatan would propose that life has the mesmerizing ebb and flow of an ocean tide, for life is habitually uncharitable in the sequencing of its moments. Such might be your experience as you read this mélange of my moments with her. Serenity accompanied by shock. A smile supplanted by a slap. Despondency and despair trailed by sprightly gist. Absurdity and anguish and amusement and anger and awe, conjoined as a frantic, ghastly five-headed beast.

Some of these relics are rife with unpleasant metaphor, evidence of the darkest imaginations she is able to conjure. Others reveal her aptitude for the overt—distilling veracity into a potent revelation. I make no claims of prowess or profundity—she would both chide and humor me should I attempt such. I suspect she has accosted you as well on your journey—for such is the calling of The Muse.

Mercifully, this is a book from which you can exercise pause to recuperate before appeasing your curiosity to resume. I've not polluted this work with context, for my aim is not catharsis, validation, or any amalgamation of ordinary motivations. My hope is that these poems and prose will echo moments of your journey and give voice to your soul. And most of all, to assure you—to prove to you—that your naked soul warrants no shame, no guilt. Never does it require apology.

Only one thing is deserving of the naked soul. Admiration.

for you

and what might have been

CONTENTS

coffee	3
Ghosts	5
signature	7
Hollow Beauty	9
desire	11
Speckled Sparrow	13
Do Don't Will Won't	15
Feat	17
scattered voices	19
Forbidden Fruit	21
Things Most Important	23
ripe	25
Young	27
bars	29
I Once Believed	31
Keep Walking	33
Light and Shadows	35
Tarnished Mirror	37
stitch	39
naked	41
seed	43
dimples	45
Emphatic	49
Threat	51
Epiphany	53
Echoes Fade Away	55
place	57
Emancipation	59
The More You	63
The One	65
The Scarlet Angel	67

Triumph	69
smudge	71
Quilt of Time	73
Romantic	75
sunset sunrise	77
bridge	79
Beauty of a Woman	81
pressure	83
Count	85
Arrow	87
run	89
embers	91
moon shines bright	93
The Grass *is* Green	95
No Vacancy	97
Cosmic Stage	99
Thief	101
Gift	103
snare	105
Lack	107
cuts of a thousand dreams	109
abandon	111
I Have Not Wept the Loss of You	113
sojourn	117
Life is Full	119
Heart of a Man	121
Yes, That Kind of Love	123
Pause	125
She Sings Only When I Am Naked	127
True	131
About the Author	135

She Sings Only When I'm Naked

coffee

drink your coffee
while it's hot

for too quickly

the steam vanishes
like wraiths on a damp morning

and flavor escapes
like a genie from an abandoned lamp

leaving but the bitter taste
of a lukewarm life

in a cup that should be
empty

♪

Ghosts

Ghosts flit across the sun
their shadows strangle its rays
shivers dispensed by heat
penetrating flesh
and ice emerges once again
within the soul.

Yesterday
they dared but the darkness of night
leaving sacred the altar of daylight
but yesterday is extinct
its only purpose to embolden their resolve
to flaunt their scorning rituals.

Brazen these ghosts have become
satisfied no longer to occupy
hallucinations in dark hallways.
They invade the domain of day
defiling its aspiration
silhouettes of doubt
lurking in laughter.

Oh, that they would clothe themselves
in flesh and blood—
no longer impervious to sword
subject to bleeding as mortals.

Perhaps, then, they would succumb
to the solitude of the grave
leaving the heart to once again
embrace the sun.

signature

a life
monumental
simple
exasperating
extraordinary
perplexing
poignant
quiet
compelling

your semiotic signature
emblazoned on my
mind
heart
soul

today
I am reminded
of the magnitude
of the magnificence
of your message
echoing
in my story

♪

Hollow Beauty

The velvet warmth of ocean breeze
Flirts with one to pause, then breathe
Nostrils filled with mist and brine
Cares fade away, repelling time

So I happened upon a find, yes rare
A perfect shell, unbroken, fair
Though void of life, its outward glow
Demanded that one must behold

Seductive lines, enchanting hues
The rough of rock, the feel of smooth
Unscathed armor, I press to ear
An empty hum, no song to hear

What creature once had called this home?
This hollow beauty which I now hold
What greater purpose drove it on
Until it awoke, too late, now gone

Shape and texture, wind and light
Pleasant pictures that darken sight
Life protected, once buried deep
Ventured forth, with fate did meet

Hollow beauty, the moment's bland
I toss the shell upon the sand
Nostrils filled with mist and brine
Cares are no more with no more time.

desire

desire
fog clouds the mind
warmth keeps soul alive
pain makes heart weep
strength to trust the tears
to forge ahead
to attain
its destined demise

Speckled Sparrow

A speckled sparrow
observing
perched
between splintered slats of peeling white fascia
framing the gable
an unintended gap
in the builder's house
a consequence of sunshine implored
rain prayers answered
blizzards forgotten.

The builder—
he would think the sparrow's refuge
insulting
embarrassing
certainly deserving of expulsion
and his mild vehemence.

But he vacated many winters ago
and his pride with him
his resting place but a dismal gray anomaly
on the distant hilltop
reflected in the eyes
of a speckled sparrow.

♪

Do Don't Will Won't

Live each day by do's and don'ts
And life will pass you by
But live each day by wills and won'ts
And passion will not die.

Live each day by do's and don'ts
And life will surely flee
But live each day by wills and won'ts
And life will set you free.

♪

Feat

He walks along the edge of gilded wood and golden sky
But touches not the heavens with his gaze
His feet are shod with nothing, but the dust of years gone by
    The voices laugh
    The crooked path
    The maidens shriek their songs of hollow praise.

He cares no longer where he goes, no yearning to be free
He questions not the meaning of his days
Trapped within the perfect world created by his dream
    The voices crowd
    The unseen shroud
    The words of poets nothing more than phrase.

                      Death by triumph, oh so cruel
                      The scourge of yet unhindered rule
                        The minions feed until they drool
                            And play him for a fool.

But Fortune frowns upon the crowds that frolic by the sea
Their chants for mercy burn like sodden coal
The envy she inspires yields but fickle fantasies
    The voices scream
    There is no dream
    Incest is the virtue they extol.

The song of lonely bird caresses silver strands of moon
Pierces deep the layers of his soul
The ghost of longing beckons soul to flee the gold lagoon
    The voices fade
    No more charade
    He journeys to a place beyond control.

♪

scattered voices

seeds of scattered voices
drift upon the breeze
like phantoms
of dandelion tufts
fertile
searching for sanctuary
whispers
enduring turbulence
passions
seeking conception
rebirth
first breath
resurrection of spirits
choir singing softly
melodies
harmonies
mysteries
of tomorrow

♪

Forbidden Fruit

Touch not the forbidden fruit
for touch leads to taste
and taste resurrects
that which is meant
to remain buried.

But the warning came too late
for I had felt its velvet
on lips and on tongue
and now knew
the bitter taste of death
was better
than no taste at all.

♪

Things Most Important

A little girl sits alone
on a park bench
between silent guardians
absorbed in news and sports
and things most important.

The little girl sits alone
and wonders when
her mind will grow up
and be bored
with watching squirrels romp and pigeons' peck
and one day desire
to be consumed
by things most important.

♪

ripe

should fortune be a verity
then such you have
as happenstance has introduced us
while I remain ripe
with a measure of sweetness still present

should grace and mercy be verities
then such we should hope for
that fate returns me to the earth
before mold and sour and squishy
replace the ripe

♪

Young

I am young
I am worn
I am not indestructible
I am invincible

I am courage
I am sorrow
I am not yet triumphant
I am terrifying

For I am young.

♪

bars

bars
    steel
    vertical
    more deadly than spears thrust deep in human flesh
    ridicule another gasp for air

bars
    adamant
    bloodstained
    more defiant than will, human or divine
    destined to conquer the spirit

bars
    taunting
    scoffing
    permit human limb and thought to pass
    forbid the heart to follow

bars
    designed
    imagined
    more potent than mamba, black and swift
    toxic teeth piercing the soul

bars

♪

I Once Believed

I once believed I was a winner
    and then I lost
    accolades absconded in the haze
    shadows of trophies
    wraiths of fickle victories.

I once believed I was a leader
    and then I fell
    collapsed with fractures unseen
    laid bare as others walked onward
    oblivious of my existence.

I once believed I was a teacher
    and then I didn't know the questions
    could not recall the answers
    pupils drifted from their desks
    as I searched for definitions.

I once believed I was a lover
    and then passion died
    lips could not embrace
    body refusing occasion for intimacy
    with the one by my side.

...

I once believed I was a warrior
    and then was violently wounded
    soul bleeding, broken
    could not be healed
    and my regiment waged war without me.

I once believed
    stars could be reached
    seas could be sailed
    wisdom should win
    love could be held
    life would make sense
    truth would prevail.

I once...

believed.

♪

Keep Walking

Two steps forward
One step backward
Two steps forward
Three steps backward.

And I find myself back where I started.

With less tread on the soles
Less water in the bottle
And hours lost that can never be replenished.

There is no certainty
the path I choose to walk
will grant passage
to desired destination.

I will encounter
cliffs too steep to scale
ravines too deep to descend
chasms too wide to cross
obstacles too massive to move.

There are moments in which
I am forced to decide:
choose a different path
or choose a different destination.

What matters most?

To keep walking.

♪

Light and Shadows

Each day the planet upon which we stir
    embraces the rays
    of a magnificent celestial enigma
whose light
    infuses the soul with fascination
    bewilders the mind with curiosity
    beckons one to embark on an adventure.

There are days on which shadows
    of clouds above
    of thoughts within
    subvert the Sol's embrace.

On such days, one may consider
it wise to believe
    fascination is fickle
    curiosity is confusing
    the adventure is too arduous to continue.

There may wisdom in such belief.

If so, I hope not to be a wise man.

I choose rather to receive
    the light
    and
    the shadows
    as gifts to treasure each day.

♪

Tarnished Mirror

The question—
    which was once a wish,
    a wish once a desire—
is now simply a thought
a flaccid rumination
    dangling like the legs
    of a discarded ragdoll
    tossed on the top shelf
    in an adolescent's closet
a shadow emerging from tarnished mirror
    each instance more fleeting
    in the moments that follow
    our partings

The cement of certainty
    permeates the sand
    in our hourglass
    future past present
    a concrete clock
    expedient explanations
    comfortable convictions
    alluring assumptions
    curiosity recoils
    as immutable impersonates clarity
    and familiarity masquerades as understanding

Yet love remains
    alive
    true
    unencumbered by supposition
    free from doubt
    intimate reflections in tarnished mirror.

I place the hourglass on the shelf next to the ragdoll
shadows and reflections retreat
    as I shift my gaze from tarnished mirror
        towards horizon
    surrendering to illusion of sanctuary
    permitting the pleasant
    choosing not the paths
        adjacent the chasms of complexity
    for I now know the answer
    to the question—
        which was once a wish,
        a wish once a desire—
    yes, I know the answer.

Be at peace with certainty.

Parting will always be a word in the last sentence
of each chapter in our story
until the day the book is closed
and opportunity for parting is no longer.

Yet, desire remains
    to write the next chapter,
    aware the sentences will be safe,
    the prose predictable,
    the themes comfortable,
    and the moments meaningful
    until arrives that day of our final parting.

When shadows no longer escape from tarnished mirror
    nor reflections grace its surface
    another will close our book
    and place it on that shelf
    where hourglass is frozen and ragdoll is forgotten.

♪

stitch

opportunity
to feel once more
sometimes imposes
the risk of
slice
snip
snap
stitch

guarantees,
there are none,
bar a lifetime of numbness
should one refuse
slice
snip
snap
stitch

♪

naked

naked

beneath the soft of down

darkness

the silence of breathing

reveals

consciousness is alive

hiding

can the flame burn again

drowning

do you hear the frantic

whispers

or is hope lost in fog

distant

searching in the empty

longing

for but a touch to bridge

the void

for but a kiss to free

our tears

♪

seed

sun
rain
soil
   cannot conceive
   yet they
warm
quench
nurture
   the seed for a season

to conceive is for seed to choose
whether to embrace
   the mystery
to risk promise
   for birth
knowing
   to embrace
   to conceive
   is to never be again

a sneering seed
   scorns veracity
   spurns consequence of delay
   yet denial of promise remains
   a lethal decision

sun
rain
soil
   are ruthless
   knowing the foolish always
   shrivel
   drown
   rot

for seed is mortal

♪

dimples

dimples
thousands
millions
inflicting faint shadows on the concrete block wall
caked in paint the color of vomit
imperceptible from a distance
but vividly visible
to the man staring at them
from a span of less than two feet
possessing the intense focus
conceived of disbelief

this legion of petite pits
a jaded audience
silently scoffing
their significance of greater import
than that of the irrelevant man
facing them
standing
as he has been so instructed

naked
arms to his side
feet spread
waiting for mandate
to issue from guard's mouth

waiting
waiting
jaw rigid
demanding his eyes
not reveal the moist of disbelief

...

guard barks
raise arms
stand on toes
grip ankles
grab and spread cheeks
bend over
incursion
flashlight beams
probing

turn around
raise balls
raise what?
pull up your goddamn balls

boxers
thin, stretched
elastic that long ago lost its virginity
tossed on concrete floor haunted
by gray veins disappearing
under forbidden doors

guard snaps
put on the goddamn boxers

as man bends to retrieve
the profane underwear
he is greeted
by petite brownish six-legged creature
intrigued by the thin stained cotton
its antennas fucking the air
vigorous, valiant
amused, perhaps, by the view

...

the man seizes wad of fabric
vain attempt to retrieve dignity
as if the shiny creature was capable
of defiling
such parody
the blasphemous creature
scurries away
awaiting opportunity
to mock the next impotent villain

left foot
right foot
stepping, pulling upwards
boxers too exhausted
to remain rigged at half-mast
fist clenching
wad of waistband
against cold torso

guard finger
hostile
dictating
directs man to plastic barrel
a cynical chiffonier
stuffed with trousers and t-shirts
ancient beige cotton
wadded, wrinkled, worn

a pile of plastic slippers
flanks the wardrobe
guard mandate to make haste
packaged in profanity
no time to ascertain the relevance of fit

...

attire designed to define
convict
miscreant
outcast
inmate
criminal

man is now adorned

guard's voice bellows
promenade beckons

metal clanging
gates locking
faces staring
desire vanishing

dimples leering

dimples sneering

prison

♪

Emphatic

Know
Everything
Nothing
All
None
Always
Never
Everybody
Nobody

Such are the words
incessantly brandished
by ignorance
by idiocy
by impotence.

♪

Threat

One is disposable
a threat to the many, who
inhale
exhale
surrendering their virgin breath
for mirages of safety—
projections of the machine
upon flickering minds.

One claims his breath for himself
perhaps but ill-fated attempt to live
in the same space
but different place
unnoticed by the many—
blinded by the machine's resolve
to assassinate
the dream
the desire
of one.

♪

Epiphany

The angst of midlife
is the struggle to accept
that some things will never change
and some things will never happen.

One may choose
to remain in this ceaseless struggle
which yields only anguish
and acrimony.

Or one may choose
to embrace abandon of things desired—
to embark upon the path on which one discovers
the things that will never change
do not matter,
and discarding the things that will never happen
invites promise
for better things to happen.

♪

Echoes Fade Away

The death of dream gives birth to blight
The heavens curse the mirth of night
The blind debate the worth of sight
    And echoes fade away
    The echoes fade away.

The vivid hues of life turn gray
The severed nerve, the knife astray
The piper drunk, no fife to play
    And echoes fade away
    The echoes fade away.

The pious break the rules of old
The poor discard the jewels of gold
The wise lament what fools have sold
    And echoes fade away
    The echoes fade away.

O Singer sing! Is song bereft?
O Giver, give! Is ember left?
O Lover, love! Is passion theft?
O Jester, jest. Thy skill is deft.

Desire drowns beneath the ice
The player doth bequeath the dice
The angry muse, the teeth of price
    And echoes fade away
    The echoes fade away.

The cast revolts, the stage, forlorn
The music stops, the pages torn
The story ends, the sages mourn
    And echoes fade away.
    The echoes fade away.

May prayer forgotten lift its wings
May voices lost find songs to sing
May barren seed feel gift of spring
    Let echoes fade away
    Let echoes fade away.

♪

place

a simple space
empty
void

invites
music
art
cuisine
boquets

vision

becomes
a place

healing
belonging
revealing
believing

creating

song
laughter
relief
joy
memories

home

♪

Emancipation

A child I was when we first met
incapable of knowing the verities of now
powerless to discern the motivations of then
a terrifying and exhilarating encounter
yearning to be accepted
fear of damnation
desperate for unconditional love.

Our relationship felt real
giving birth to bond
simple
mysterious
serious
reassuring.

Then conviction eradicated mystery
the presumption of understanding
the pretense of experience
the charade of creeds
the prayers of piety.

Yet, the presence of your love remained true
and I proclaimed my love for you
in prayers and blemished deed.

Then conviction gave way to ambiguity
gave way to choices
gave way to danger
gave way to turmoil
gave way to desperation.

...

Yet still I clung, frantic to believe.

Until, no longer able to grasp, I let go.

And I died.

In the void
I could not see
I could not hear
I could not speak
I could not touch
I could not taste
I could not
dared not
believe.

For you abandoned me
a pretentious thought I know
some say heretical
and one I think no longer.

Today I do not proclaim
your presence to multitudes.
Yet, I believe that you are
and that is enough.

For knowledge does not reveal truth
nor does expectation produce hope
nor does experience prove faith.

I question not where the journey leads
for it is a mystery
not meant for mortals to discover.

I simply ask for strength
    to take another step
for grace
    to extend forgiveness
for courage
    to be human
and for imperfect love
    to vanquish fear
    and kindle hope
wherever I may roam.

♪

The More You...

The more you laugh, the more you live

The more you live, the more you cry

The more you cry, the more you see

You can't take life too seriously.

♪

The One

There are those who pass through life
leaving but a faint trail of bitter dreams.

Some pass their days
acquiring that
which they cannot keep
and keeping that
which was meant to give.

Others live loudly, saying little
while many live hollow
and expect nothing.

And then there is
the one
living life in its fullness
giving more in a simple smile
than most have ambit to receive.

In waves of difficulty
in currents of injustice
the one
remains true to hope
unwavering in love
on sail to destination that beckons
the soul to know its Creator.

This intrepid does not fancy fate
nor tempt it
being secure in manner few can fathom.

For the one
has discovered their heart
and the One
for which it was created.

♪

The Scarlet Angel

The scarlet angel drinks alone
before appointed time
his mission harsh: preserve the throne
    he knows that grace
    requires haste
    and promise, e'er the caveat
    is far the greater crime.

The naked child sleeps alone
beyond his time to wake
his memories trapped inside the drone
    of truth that lies
    to stifle cries
    creating neon fantasies
    lest angst begin to quake.

The scarlet angel comes as thief
for moon will soon demand
to harvest fears that yield belief
    to give the gift
    he must be swift
    regret, the threat, cannot succumb
    lest demons seize command.

The naked child stirs so slight
veracity to kiss
forbidden by a searing light
    his tears are lost
    the line is crossed
    and brazen embryos of hope
    are lost in the abyss

The scarlet angel curses sword
as he withdraws the blade
a lonely heart cannot be lord
 to feign alive
 form must survive
 and purpose, oft the obstacle,
 must only be charade.

The naked child, eyes unveiled,
as angry moon does flee
the curse of thunder now revealed
 the ocean's roar
 is heard no more
 as passion, frail, but gasping still
 is drowned in churning sea.

The scarlet angel drinks once more
this time to numb the mind
his perfect aim has won the war
 the corpse will live
 the flesh will give
 and soul, the casualty of faith,
 a tombstone for the blind.

Now I arise to meet the day
aware that something's gone
no matter now, the world is gray
 the act begins
 there are no sins
 and promise, once the caveat
 will sing no more its song.

♪

Triumph

Do not lose heart.

The destination
chosen by the majority
is not inevitable.

Choose wisely
your words.

Invest wisely
your time.

Hold fast to your humanity.

Anchor your courage
knowing this:

Truth will triumph.

Love will conquer evil.

♪

smudge

smudge of moon
a perfect blemish
on royal blue dusk
hovering above dunes
sand the red of open wounds
furrowed by fingers
of a lazy wind
too bored to yawn
as scorpions cast exaggerated shadows
the duel to death
a dramatic spectacle
entertaining a lone spectator
perched atop the pinnacle
of a clean carcass
former dwelling of a soul now lost
illuminated
by the smudge of moon

Quilt of Time

The quilt of time lies tattered
on worn wood floor
stains of black from red of life
shards of glass scattered
once a crystal shield
protecting his sepia memory
of her.

One chosen splinter
the angel of mercy
emancipating his sorrow
leaving lifeless form
forsaken
upon the quilt of time.

♪

Romantic

The romantic
who
is oblivious to his condition—
whether due to ignorance
or denial—
still enhances the world with unexpected delights.

Should he become aware of his condition,
he may consider it a curse,
an eccentricity,
or a calling.

However, the wise simply smile
knowing it is none of these things.

It is simply his immutable nature.

♪

sunset sunrise

yesterday's sunset
    cannot be resurrected
    its splendor vanished
    satiated rays buried
    beneath eaves of night
    the brief moment
    alive only in memory
    of unhurried observer

tomorrow's sunrise
    cannot be conjured
    its brilliance unconceived
    embryonic rays buried
    beneath the promise of time
    the brief hope
    alive only in the pleas
    of a desperate sinner

♪

bridge

concrete pillars
pierce the earth
converge on stone
laced with steel and the resolve of human sweat
garner nary a thought
by those who pass on bridge above
intent on destination
heedless of respect
for the road on which they travel
made possible
by concrete pillars
laced with steel and the resolve of human sweat

Beauty of a Woman

The beauty of a woman
Is plain for all to see
On glossy page and pageant stage
We want what cannot be

But strip away the luscious hair
Vanish lash and brow
Add some faded lines of care
Then pale the skin somehow

The simple mind can only see
What common people dread
And experts jostle to explain
What's better left unsaid

But wise the man who treasures
What misfortune dares reveal
For the beauty of a woman
Is a beauty that is concealed

Strength that makes the warrior bow
Song that sets men free
Lust for life most never know
While chasing empty dreams

Eyes that shine like silver moons
On vast Caribbean seas
Words that heal the heart of wounds
Then linger like gentle breeze

Fire burns within her breast
Oh Passion! that must give
Satisfies what flesh can't feel
Ignites the soul to live

Though one may tame a tiger
Or ride the wild steed
One cannot capture beauty
He can only grasp his need

The beauty of a woman
Not meant for all to see
Lies far beyond the reach of men
It is the power to believe.

♪

pressure

pressure
too high
the risk
of stroke

pressure
too low
the risk
of shock

pressure
no more
the risk
is gone

pressure
just right
the risk
of living

♪

Count

Desire is deep in the human heart
to not be counted,
but to count
in the sum of a great thing.

But the world is ruled by those
who demand
that others be counted,
numbered,
expected to produce
things that count little
but for those who rule.

Thus the person who listens to their heart
and determines to count
for something more than a number,
must know their value,
must refuse the lie,
must resist the temptation
to believe that one must rule
to count.

♪

Arrow

Worn and weathered
    weak and bent
    frayed by countless wars 'neath dreary skies

    Lone and tired
    dull and gaunt
    the arrow lay in quiver want to die

Wounded warrior
    tired and spent
    scarred by countless wars and many woes

    Lone yet yearning
    alive alert
    bends quiet knee to hide from vaunted foes

Chance and promise
    seize the day
    lone arrow taut in warrior's battered bow

    Will sun arise
    as arrow flies
    fate shall reveal that only one will know

♪

run

run

    rue the moment of pungent conception
    laced with the debris of affection
    invoking hope without trace of breath

run

    abscond to the dell of denial
    drink in the hollow air
    void of torment and toil

run

    halt not for the dawn of confession
    taunting the brazen horizon
    as vapors of promise vanish in empty rays

run

♪

embers

nestled atop a mound of ash
embers smolder
tinged with the same dull white
accosting my temples

I ponder opportunity
to retrieve another split of timber
one more time
as I have done on countless occasions
then gently positioning dead oak
upon the dusty mound
before the vanishing
of ember glow

for spark is not eternal

yet
I pause
unconvinced
might truth reveal the gift of timber
is but the bane
that extinguishes opportunity

leaning in
I exhale
gently
the embers smile
the promise of resurrection
revealed in grateful glow

but no longer am I a fool
to believe the blaze
will be as impressive
as before

though timber remains
my stash is small
and warmth is no longer
desired

so I gaze
peacefully
the embers
flickering
gasping
reflections in weary eyes
waiting for ash
to honor my soul

♪

moon shines bright

moon shines bright
on somber night
yet magic glow will pass

whether dawn takes aim
with rays or rain
may hope find strength to last

♪

The Grass *is* Green

The grass is green, or so they say
Thus green we come to know
No matter that the grass is brown
The planted seeds still grow.

The grass is dead, in need of rain
But this we cannot see
The devout demand we all conform
Thus truth is brown is green.

So when the heretic proclaims
That brown is brown and green
Is something else, we ridicule
To what we know, we cling.

Then rain falls on thirsty earth
Brings life to tender reed
But life is lost in vacant eyes
For brown is our belief.

No Vacancy

NO VACANCY
blinking sign
glaring
at burdened traveler
beneath sheets of rain.

Neon angels
dance
in his mind
anxious to follow
shadows of forgotten dreams
spiral down the corridor of steel
to their heavenly home.

♪

Cosmic Stage

Some claim marriage is a covenant.
Others say, but a contract.
Some might consider it an experiment.
And others an inquisition.

Some suppose marriage is the
culmination of abiding affection.
And not a few believe it is
necessary to curtail concupiscence.

Across histories and cultures,
no other relationship has proven
capable of invoking the amplitude
of human emotion with such ferocity.

I suspect marriage is simply a rehearsal
for some comedic role one must perform
on some cosmic stage in the afterlife.

♪

Thief

The thief is a singer of truth
    perverted
    by defiant drums
    contempt for harmony and melody and meter.

Like fingers of thirsty trees
    greedy
    for water in fertile earth
    his twisted songs infiltrate mind and soul.

Incessant, his chants lure the soul
    ensnared
    in caverns of pompous dreams
    disguising shattered skeletons and rotting flesh.

Let fury inflame your spirit
    revolt
    wield the brazen sword
    thrust it deep into his skull.

Slay the liar and live.

♪

Gift

You have been given the gift—
the gift of life.

Do not be timid. Or proper.
Rip off the wrapping paper.

I implore—
do not place your gift in a display cabinet
where it might be admired once a year.

Rather
Unleash your gift.
Eschew bashful. Shun caution.
Brandish your gift with gusto!

Use it in the blazing heat.
Use it in the terrifying storm.
Use it while the sun soars.
Use it as the moon rises.

Keep using your gift
even when it's wearing out
and must be held together
with duct tape and superglue and
rubber bands and wire strands.

Use not your gift for spectacle.
Waste not your gift on only
the accumulation of experiences.

For your gift—the gift of life—
is for creating.

Creating hope.
Creating laughter.
Creating trails and bridges.
Creating questions.
Creating sails. And wings.
Creating peace.
Creating joy.
Creating connection.

Creating... life.

Yes, life is for creating.

And you,
yes you,
you have been given the gift—
the gift of life.

♪

snare

the angry gift
given in haste
deceives the feeble mind

the joyous occasion
but a snare for the fool
that concedes the throne
for accord

♪

Lack

The grass was never green enough
Home was never clean enough
Repairs were never fast enough
Vacations never long enough.

The house was never big enough
Income not secure enough
Savings never high enough
Plans were never sure enough.

Our time was never quite enough
My words did not reveal enough
My actions never meant enough
Our union never strong enough.

Then, one day, she had
had enough
of not enough
and left me with my lack.

Years have passed
and so have tears
and I have come to have enough
though still I live with lack.

And, in moments random—
invaded by erratic curiosity—
the silent hope arises:

That she no longer lives with
not enough.

cuts of a thousand dreams

death
by the cuts of a thousand dreams
such welcome emancipation

if but mercy
such incisions mirrored
the mild effects
of serrated blade
penetrating ligament and sinew
bursting free
crimson nectar of life
birthing hope
for a brighter horizon

for random souls
dreams
vaunted virtuous sincere serene
are but ruse
antics of celestial deity
slicing soul into a thousand strands

yet chained
to another breath

yet denied
the promise of desire

♪

abandon

the voice of freedom crackles
on frequencies
that cannot be heard
searching the heart for a crevice
until the storms pass
and one forsakes
the pursuit of happiness
that enslaves the soul

♪

I Have Not Wept the Loss of You

I have not yet wept the loss of you
of us
not for absence of tears
    denied by paralysis
    accruing with passage of time
not for lack of what ifs
    though still unconvinced
    I possess courage ample
    to circumvent self-inflicted uncertainty

impromptu tokens
    never predictable
    never unwelcome
        volleyball game
            a player's grinning glance
            aimed at lone admirer
        moronic pedestrian
            clueless, impeding
            affixed on New York sidewalk
        stranger resolute
            wielding crutches
            conquering the path ahead
        moonlight dancing
            taunting gentle waves
            on Lake Michigan shore
        dangly soft rabbit
            in toy store window
            in grandchild crib
    reminders
    the unshed reservoir remains deep

...

    I still attempt endeavors
    of sort to foster health
    defiance of declining physique included
        amusing a spectator named Good Luck
        I'm now a decade beyond halfway to 110
            a discarded aim
        I glance across the gym
            a wraith of your visage
            exhilaration of curiosity
            now absent
    unfamiliar faces
    the clink and clank of weights
    another drop collects in the pool

I have acquired a smirk
    I wish as pure as yours
        never condescending
        just simple acknowledgement
        of the absurdities in life

destiny?
    the word forever elicits a smile
    breakfast with a purported atheist
    I think you would smile
    to discover I invited
        doubt
    to be a guest
    at my masquerade of evidence
    though elaborate masks
    conceal the identities of revelers
    and the mystery of doubt's beauty remains

...

your letter
    parting
    tender
    aching
    prophesying
        this moment would come
    a treasure
    in envelope I no longer open

last night I lay in bed
    solitaire
    moon obscured by clouds
    moist eyes
    restraint
    I did not weep
    perhaps some day
    but likely not

for I cherish
    this reservoir
    knowing I will not drown
    only drift
    a familiarity more desired
    than traversing barren desert
    for within these waters deep
    swim countless smiles
    and I fear that opening the dam
    would expel them
    into the channel of regret
    forever escaping my soul

this is why
I have not yet wept the loss of you.

♪

sojourn

one may sojourn
alone
on barren path
o'er crest
through deep ravine
yet not know
loneliness

the serene soul
pulsing
perceiving
the Creator's soliloquies
resounding
resonating
in chambers
deep
in heavens
beyond

♪

Life is Full

Life is full of sunshine

Life is full of shit

So thank God for your blessings

And don't forget your wit.

♪

Heart of a Man

The heart of a man
is the heart of a boy
for such hearts are not designed to age
as is the mind
and soul
and hearts of women.

The play of boys to battle
is but nature's attempt to steel the mind
to wield the sword
to don the armor
that guards the heart.

The years beyond the boy
betray the security of manly armor
revealing the perils of heart exposed.

For resilience
is anchored in the heart of a woman
but only in the minds of men.

And aspiration
is anchored in the minds of women
but in a man,
remains alive only in his heart.

♪

Yes, That Kind of Love

love
yes, that kind of love

but for a moment
    fingers gentle
    drifting
    through sepia strands
    atop the crown
    before the gray
    before the gloom

love
yes, that kind of love

but for a moment
    hands entwined
    knowing
    a warmth assured
    a grasp secure
    before the clave
    before the wound

love
yes, that kind of love

but for a moment
    lips supple
    seeking
    the delicate delight
    of a lover
    before the cave
    before the doom

...

love
yes, that kind of love

but for a moment
    eyes enlightened
    discerning
    the silent soul
    truth unshackled
    before the stray
    before the brume

love
yes, that kind of love

but for a moment
    hearts pulsing
    becoming
    a flawless cadence
    eternal exhilaration
    before the slay
    before the tomb

love
yes, that kind of love

but for a moment

♪

Pause

Pause.

Breathe deeply.

Observe
closely
the world surrounding you.

You will find beauty
gently smiling at you
from the most
delighted faces.

♪

She Sings Only When I Am Naked

She has the voice of an angel
    this I will not say
    for I have not heard
    an angelic voice
    whether in colossal choir from on high
    of from lone winged creature
    heralding news of any sort.

Angelic voices are magnificent
    I've been informed
    and I have been impressed
    once—maybe twice—
    by attempts of imaginative humans
    emulating the alleged anthems
    of seraphs and cherubs and a heavenly chorus.

Yet, I refuse insipid metaphors
    to depict her voice,
    for concern it would degrade my authority
    on this matter,
    and for graver concern that implying resemblance
    to any other creature
    is patronizing and perilous.

I do wager
    her voice would cause angelic hosts
    to cease
    and listen
    for hers is a voice like no other.

The grandest of cathedrals
    would revere for eternity
    any moment in which her songs
    resounded within its sanctum.

But that moment will never ensue,
    this I know,
    for such is not her ambition.

In the moments of her choosing,
she sings only to an audience of one.

She lacks not confidence, knowing—
    as well as I—
    hers is a voice
    stupendous
    soothing
    haunting
    poignant
    probing
    provocative
    disturbing
    glorious
    but she seeks not acclaim,
    only consummation.

Unpredictable are our liaisons
    the season matters not
    she chooses at will or whim
    invading my space
    without regard for anticipation or dread.

...

Her presence
> mesmerizing, maddening
> obliterates wisdom
> the tick and the tock stop
> oh, I so yearn to hear her sing.

I acquiesce
I disrobe
> removing all that makes me
> think what I am
> removing all that makes me
> feel who I am
> for she will not sing until I am unabashedly
> naked.

My final breath will arrive
> when I have tired of her indescribable song
> when I no longer implore her ephemeral presence.

Jealous? Yes, I am.

Yet still I hope that someday
> you...
> you will experience her voice—
> stupendous
> soothing
> haunting
> poignant
> probing
> provocative
> disturbing
> glorious—
> the ballad of truth.

The song of the muse.

♪

True

May your heart remain true.

May its capacity for compassion
ever increase.

May the strength of its pulse
never decrease.

May the power of its love
forever birth hope
wherever you are.

May your heart remain true.

♪

One thing only
is deserving of
the naked soul.

Admiration.

♪

About the Author

Christopher Garrett is an author, musician, artist, father, grandfather, son, brother, friend, enthusiast, and sojourner. He aims to be a paragon of excellence, a provocateur of new perspectives, a purveyor of hope, a presence of peaceful energy, and a catalyst for creativity.

You can experience Christopher's additional creative works on his website and other platforms.

www.christophergarrett.co

তাই কেৱল মই উলংগ হৈ থাকোঁতে গান গায়

Also by Christopher Garrett

The Creator Creed

creatorcreed.com

www.ingramcontent.com/pod-product-compliance
Lightning Source LLC
Chambersburg PA
CBHW020536080526
44583CB00013B/886